W9-BNU-733

Rodgers & Hammerstein

BIRTHDAY BOOK

Rodgers & Hammerstein

BIRTHDAY BOOK

A celebration of the world's
best loved musicals

Compiled by Bert Fink

Harry N. Abrams, Inc., Publishers

Produced in association with The Rodgers & Hammerstein Organization

Mary Martin in The Sound of Music *(1959)*

Editor: Robert Morton
Designer: Liz Trovato
Photo Editor: John Crowley

ISBN: 0–8109–3770–0

Copyright © 1993 The Rodgers & Hammerstein Organization

Published in 1993 by Harry N. Abrams, Incorporated, New York
A Times Mirror Company
All rights reserved. No part of the contents of this book
may be reproduced without the written permission of the publisher

Printed and bound in Japan

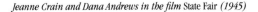

Jeanne Crain and Dana Andrews in the film State Fair *(1945)*

A Note to the Reader

Richard Rodgers and Oscar Hammerstein II collaborated on nine stage musicals, one television musical, and one movie musical (apart from screen adaptations of their stage successes) in their seventeen-year partnership. Both men had flourishing careers before their first show, *Oklahoma!*, was produced in 1943, and Rodgers continued to create new works with others from Hammerstein's death in 1960 until shortly before his own, in 1979.

This birthday book concerns itself with dates and milestones pertaining only to the Rodgers & Hammerstein musicals. Even from that finite scope one could reach out in ever growing circles of names and places, so I have attempted to draw some lines.

Included here are: the dates of birth, marriage, and death for Richard Rodgers and Oscar Hammerstein II; the dates of birth of well-known performers and other artists who played significant roles in the history of Rodgers & Hammerstein musicals, along with their pertinent, related Broadway and Hollywood credits.

As for the musicals themselves, the book includes the opening date for every: world premiere; original Broadway run; original London run; U.S. national tour; movie world premiere; and noteworthy U.S. revival. Also included are the Broadway premieres for the plays and musicals produced but not written by Rodgers & Hammerstein. Closing dates and performance data are included in the opening date entry unless the run exceeded 1,000 performances, in which case the closing date receives its own entry.

—— Bert Fink

Participants in a salute to Rodgers and Hammerstein broadcast live on television on March 28, 1954 were: from upper left, Tony Martin and Rosemary Clooney, Florence Henderson and Gordon MacRae, Mary Martin and Ezio Pinza, Patricia Morison and Yul Brynner; second row, Jan Clayton and John Raitt, Bill Hayes and Janice Rule; first row, Ed Sullivan, Groucho Marx, Jack Benny, Charlie McCarthy and Edgar Bergen, and, forefront, Rodgers and Hammerstein.

Introduction

In 1952 Oscar Hammerstein II surprised his long-time friend and collaborator Richard Rodgers with a special birthday greeting in the June issue of *Town & Country* magazine. Not to be outdone, Rodgers a year later turned the tables on his partner in the same periodical.

Happy Birthday, Dear Dick

Dear Dick:

Becoming fifty is only a mild achievement. It is an age neither old enough nor young enough to deserve more than polite congratulations. A better reason for doffing one's hat to you is the fact that at the age of fifty you are Dick Rodgers. I think this is a very good thing to be. You have used your half century well. You have acquired and held onto a very fine wife, and you have helped her raise two very fine daughters. You have been writing plays since you were seventeen years old, and an amazing number of them have been hits. For these plays you have composed all kinds of melodies: sweet and warm and hot and dramatic and humorous and rhythmic. These have not been born without industrious effort. You have, nevertheless, told me that you feel a positive pleasure in the actual creation of a song, and this is not an experience shared by many writers. Most of them, like me, have to sweat and grind and worry, and postpone their enjoyment until they consider the job finished.

Most of all, I am congratulating you because your accomplishments and your successes are so thoroughly savored by you. Too many people cling too long to the grief that comes from failure, and too few people cling long enough to the thrill that comes from success. I congratulate you for your capacity to enjoy all the lovely things you have written, and I thank you — on behalf of all the world — for the enjoyment that all the rest of us have had from them. I thank you most particularly on my own behalf for consenting to the marriage of your notes with my words for the past decade. In two more decades you will be seventy, and I will be seventy-seven. I have always thought it would be nice to retire at about that time, so I am warning you that when you are seventy, you'll have to find a new boy. From then on I shall sit in the audience, continue to love your music, and to hate his lyrics.

Meanwhile, on this particular birthday, be happy.

Oscar

P.S. If by some chance this letter is published in *Town & Country* before your birthday arrives, then save your copy and read it over on June 28. I never write more than one birthday letter a year to anyone.

Oscar Hammerstein II

I HAVE SEEN A LINE OF SNOW-WHITE
DRAWN ACROSS AN EVENING
I HAVE SEEN DIVINE, UNSPOKEN WORDS
SHINING IN A LOVER'S EYE.
I HAVE SEEN MOONLIGHT ON A MOUNTAIN
SILVER AND COOL AND STILL.
I HAVE HEARD CHURCH BELLS FAINTLY ECHOING
OVER A DISTANT HILL.
CLOSE ENOUGH TO BEAUTY I HAVE
AND, IN ALL THE WHOLE WIDE
HERE'S THE SWEETEST SIGHT THAT I HAVE
ONE OLD COUPLE, WALKING HAND IN
WORDS BY O.H.
D.H.

Happy Birthday, Dear Oscar

Dear Oscar:

I wish to write a few words on the occasion of your fifty-eighth birthday and, as I begin, I realize that it is others rather than you who are to be congratulated the most. I congratulate your wife for having been allowed to be close to you for twenty-four years. I congratulate your nearly countless children for the love and guidance you have given them, and your friends for your help and touching loyalty. Most of all, I think, I congratulate the world for having your words in all their humor and wisdom and emotion and humanity. Finally, and with pride, I congratulate myself on this partnership, this collaboration, this friendship with you. Stay well.

Your affectionate admirer,

Dick

Richard Rodgers

January

1 2 3

Yul Brynner and Mary Beth Peil in the 1985 Broadway revival of The King and I

4 5 6 7

1980
Broadway theatre marquees are blacked out for one minute at curtain time on Saturday evening in memory of Richard Rodgers, who had died at the age of 77 the previous Sunday.

1985
Yul Brynner begins his farewell engagement as the King of Siam in *The King and I* at the Broadway Theatre. The production sets a new Broadway record for advance ticket sales purchased in a single week, grossing $1,541,547.

8   9   10   11

1954
Richard Rodgers receives
an honorary Doctorate
in Music and Oscar
Hammerstein II an
honorary Doctorate
in Letters from their
alma mater, Columbia
University.

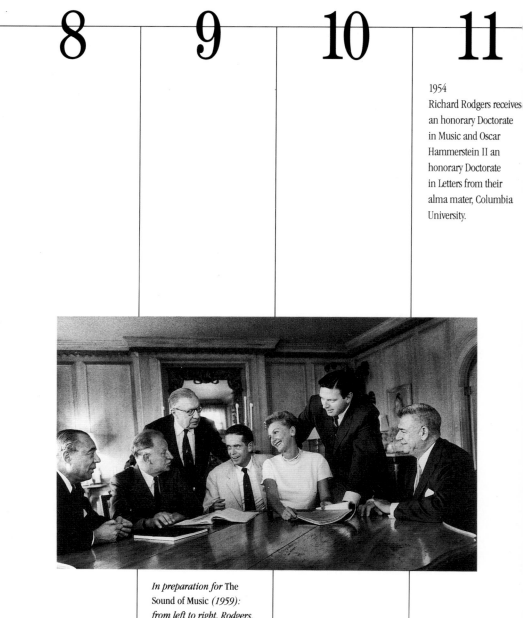

In preparation for The
Sound of Music *(1959):
from left to right, Rodgers,
Russel Crouse, Howard
Lindsay, Vincent J.
Donehue, Mary Martin,
Theodore Bikel, and
Hammerstein*

12 13 14 15

1967
The Sound of Music finishes its run at the Palace Theatre, London, after six years and 2,385 performances — the longest running American musical in British theatrical history.

Celeste Holm and Lee Dixon in Oklahoma! *(1943)*

16　17　18　19

1954

South Pacific closes on
Broadway after five years
and 1,925 performances.
Original cast member
Myron McCormick, who
played Luther Billis, leads
the final-night crowd in
"Auld Lang Syne," and in
a symbolic gesture the curtain remains unlowered.
At its closing *South Pacific*
is the second-longest running show in Broadway
history, right behind
Oklahoma!

*Myron McCormick (fifth
from left, arms folded)
and chorus during the
making of the original
Broadway cast album for*
South Pacific *(1949)*

20   21   22   23

1988

The first London revival of *South Pacific* opens at the Prince of Wales Theatre. Mary Martin, star of the original Broadway and London productions, attends this opening night and afterward tells the press: "I have never seen the show before — not even the movie. It was a very special and touching experience."

24

1950
Samuel Taylor's comedy
The Happy Time, presented
by Rodgers & Hammerstein,
opens at the Plymouth
Theatre, New York, and
runs for 614 performances.

25

26

1905
Maria Augusta Kutschera
Trapp (Maria von Trapp) is
born aboard a train in the
Tirol, Austria. The story of
her early life serves as the
inspiration for *The Sound
of Music.*

1931
Lynn Riggs' folk-play
Green Grow the Lilacs, the
inspiration for *Oklahoma!,*
opens at the Guild Theatre,
New York, where it runs for
64 performances.

27

*Mary Martin (far left)
visits Maria von Trapp
(third from right) and
members of the Trapp
family shortly before
rehearsals begin on*
The Sound of Music *(195?*

28   29   30   31

1917
John Raitt, the original
Billy Bigelow in *Carousel,*
is born in Santa Ana,
California.

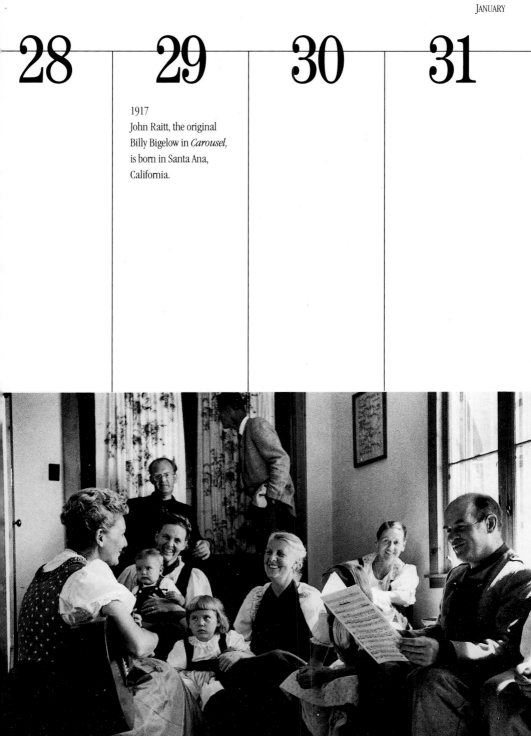

February

1   2   3

Rodgers and Hammerstein
at the St. James Theatre,
New York (1951)

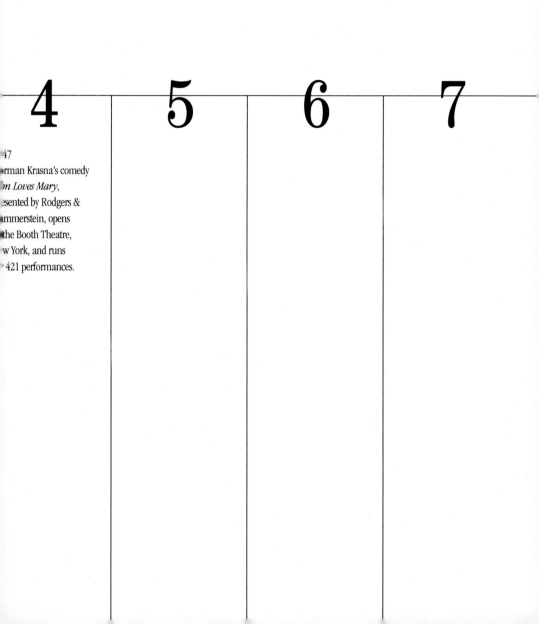

4
5
6
7

47
rman Krasna's comedy
n Loves Mary,
esented by Rodgers &
mmerstein, opens
the Booth Theatre,
w York, and runs
421 performances.

8

9

10

11

*Winners at the sixth
annual Tony Awards
(1952): from left to righ.
Hammerstein, Gertrude
Lawrence, Rodgers, Hele.
Hayes, Phil Silvers, Judy
Garland, Yul Brynner*

12 13 14 15

16   17   18   19

1953

The national tour of *South Pacific* begins a one-week engagement at the Tower Theatre, Atlanta. In response to the song "You've Got To Be Carefully Taught," members of the Georgia State Legislature issue a vehement protest and introduce a bill to outlaw entertainment works having "an underlying philosophy inspired by Moscow."

1956

Twentieth Century Fox releases the movie version of *Carousel* starring Shirley Jones and Gordon MacRae.

1976

At the 18th annual Grammy Awards in Los Angeles, the original 1943 Broadway cast album of *Oklahoma!* is inducted into the Grammy Hall of Fame.

Featured in a scene from the film Carousel *(1956) are: left to right, Audrey Christie, Gordon MacRae, Shirley Jones, Barbara Ruick*

20   21   22   23

1965
A television remake of
Cinderella starring Lesley
Ann Warren premieres on
the CBS-TV network;
it is broadcast eight more
times through February 3,
1974.

*a scene from the televi-
on remake of* Cinderella
*965) are: left to right,
arbara Ruick, Lesley Ann
arren, Pat Carroll, Jo Van
eet*

24

1950
Graham Greene's drama
The Heart of the Matter,
presented by Rodgers &
Hammerstein, opens at the
Wilbur Theatre, Boston,
where it closes two weeks
later.

25

26

1945
USO Camp Shows Inc.,
under the direction of
Reginald and Ted
Hammerstein (respectively,
brother and cousin to
lyricist Oscar), launches
a nine-month tour of
Oklahoma! for members
of the U.S. Armed Forces
stationed in the Pacific
theater.

1951
The world premiere of
The King and I is pre-
sented at the Shubert
Theatre, New Haven.

1989
*Jerome Robbins'
Broadway,* an anthology
of the director/choreogra-
pher's musicals, opens at
the Imperial Theatre,
New York, and features
"The Small House of Uncle
Thomas" ballet from
The King and I. Susan
Kikuchi, daughter of
original cast member
Yuriko, dances her
mother's role of Eliza.

27

1961
The national tour of *The
Sound of Music* starring
Florence Henderson begins
at the Riviera Theatre,
Detroit, and plays in 35
cities before closing at the
O'Keefe Center, Toronto,
on November 23, 1963.

28   29

Florence Henderson in the national tour of The Sound of Music *(1961)*

March

1

2

1965
Twentieth Century Fox
premieres the movie
version of *The Sound of
Music,* directed by Robert
Wise and starring Julie
Andrews and Christopher
Plummer, at the Rivoli
Theatre, New York, where it
plays for a record-setting
93 weeks. The movie's ini-
tial U.S. release lasts four-
and-a-half years, and from
1966 to 1972 *The Sound
of Music* is cited by *Variety*
as "All-Time Box Office
Champion." It remains
the most popular movie
musical ever made.

3

4 5 6 7

1930
Richard Rodgers marries
Dorothy Feiner.

1945
At the 18th annual
Academy Awards, "It Might
As Well Be Spring" from
State Fair receives the
Oscar for Song of the Year.

1949
The world premiere of
South Pacific is presented
at the Shubert Theatre,
New Haven.

*Christopher Plummer sings
to the children in the film*
The Sound of Music *(1965)*

8

9

10

11

1919
Up Stage and Down, an
amateur musical comedy
written to benefit the
Infants Relief Society,
features the first songs
written together by
17-year-old composer
Richard C. Rodgers and
24-year-old lyricist Oscar
Hammerstein II.

1943
The world premiere of
Rodgers & Hammerstein's
first musical *Away We Go!*
is presented at the Shubert
Theatre, New Haven. At
its next stop, Boston, it
acquires a new showstop-
per, which becomes the
title song when it opens on
Broadway as *Oklahoma!*

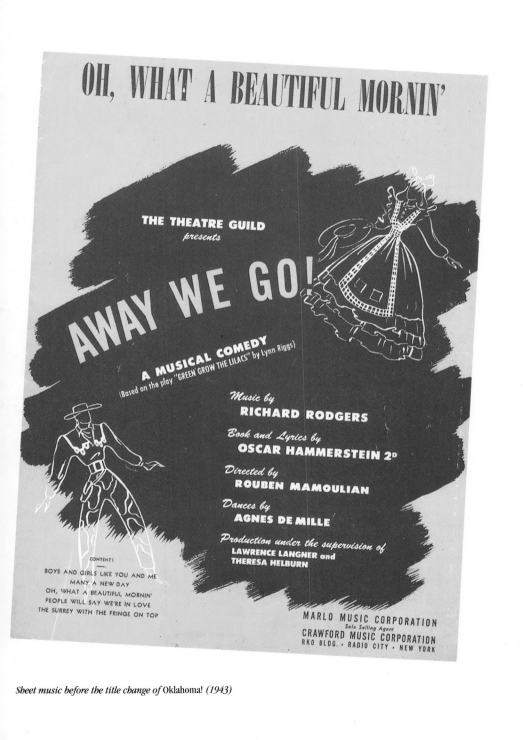

Sheet music before the title change of Oklahoma! *(1943)*

Ann-Margret and Pat Boone in the film remake of State Fair *(1962)*

12

1921
Gordon Albert MacRae
born in East Orange,
New Jersey. His screen
appearances include Curly
in *Oklahoma!* (1955)
and Billy Bigelow in
Carousel (1956).

13

14

1929
Oscar Hammerstein II
marries Dorothy
Blanchard Jacobson.

15

1962
Twentieth Century Fox
releases a remake of the
movie *State Fair*, directed
by Jose Ferrer, and starring
Pat Boone, Bobby Darin,
and Ann-Margret.

*Oscar and Dorothy
Hammerstein*

16

17

18

19

1958
Twentieth Century Fox
releases the movie version
of *South Pacific* starring
Rossano Brazzi and
Mitzi Gaynor.

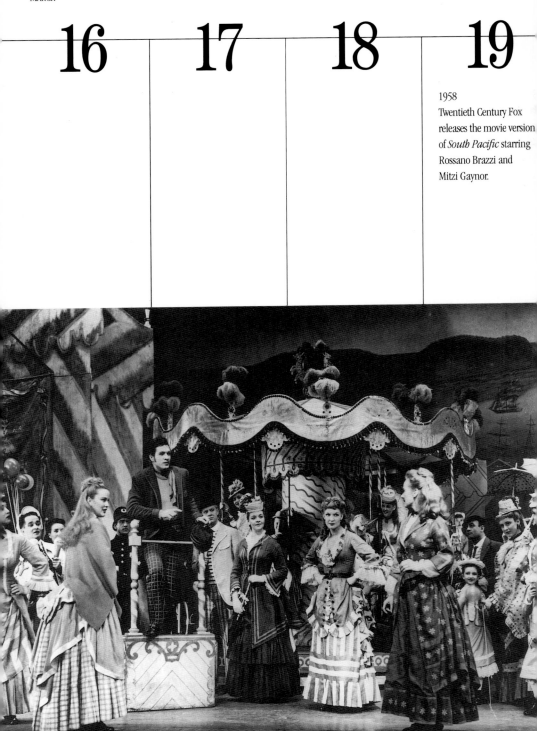

20   21   22   23

954
he King and I closes
n Broadway after
246 performances.

1945
The world premiere of
Carousel is presented
at the Shubert Theatre,
New Haven.

1954
The national tour of
The King and I starring
Patricia Morison begins
at the Community Theatre,
Hershey, Pennsylvania,
and tours for 42 weeks,
visiting 30 cities before
closing at the Shubert
Theatre, Philadelphia, on
December 17, 1955.

rincipals in Carousel
*945): left to right, Jean
arling, John Raitt, Jean
isto, Jan Clayton

24

1960
Flower Drum Song opens
at the Palace Theatre,
London, and runs for
464 performances.

25

*Julie Andrews,
Hammerstein, and
Rodgers prepare for the
television premiere of*
Cinderella *(1957)*

26

1968
At Philharmonic (now
Avery Fisher) Hall in
New York, Skitch
Henderson and Richard
Rodgers conduct the
New York Philharmonic
Symphony Orchestra and
an all-star cast in the
silver anniversary concert
of *Oklahoma!*

27

1957
At the 29th annual
Academy Awards
The King and I
receives five Oscars,
including Best Actor
(Yul Brynner).

1990
Broadway's 46th Street
Theatre is renamed the
Richard Rodgers Theatre,
housing a permanent
exhibit devoted to the
composer's life and works

28

954

eneral Foods sponsors a
)-minute tribute to
odgers & Hammerstein
oadcast on the NBC, CBS,
3C, and DuMont networks
multaneously. Hosted by
ary Martin and featuring
gments from *Oklahoma!,*
ate Fair, Carousel,
'egro, South Pacific,
e King and I and
e and Juliet with many
embers of the original
sts, it is also highlighted
special appearances
om Jack Benny, Groucho
arx, Edgar Bergen and
arlie McCarthy,
Sullivan, and
odgers & Hammerstein.

29

1943
Marlo Music Corp.
publishes "The P.T. Boat
Song. (Steady as You Go)".
Written by Rodgers &
Hammerstein, the song
is dedicated to the officers
and men of the Motor
Torpedo Boats, and all
royalties go to the Navy
Relief Society.

1951
The King and I opens
at the St. James Theatre,
New York.

30

1952
At the sixth annual Tony
Awards *The King and I*
receives five, including
Best Musical of the Year.

31

1934
Shirley Jones is born in
Smithtown, Pennsylvania.
After making her stage
debut in the chorus of
South Pacific and appear-
ing in *Me and Juliet* on
Broadway and on tour, she
wins the coveted role of
Laurey in the movie
version of *Oklahoma!*
(1955) and follows that as
Julie Jordan in the movie
of *Carousel* (1956).

1943
Oklahoma! opens at
the St. James Theatre,
New York.

1957
Rodgers & Hammerstein's
only musical for television,
Cinderella starring Julie
Andrews, is broadcast
live on CBS-TV before an
estimated audience of
107 million.

April

1

2

3

1851
Mongkut is crowned King
of Siam. In 1862, he hires
English army widow Anna
Leonowens to serve as gov-
erness to his 82 children.
Her memoirs, novelized
by Margaret Landon as
*Anna and the King of
Siam*, serve as the basis
for *The King and I.*

*Mary Martin and Ezio
Pinza in* South Pacific
(1949)

4 5 6 7

1949
South Pacific opens at
the Majestic Theatre,
New York.

1954
A post-Broadway run of
Me and Juliet opens
at the Shubert Theatre,
Chicago, closing there on
May 29, 1954.

8

9

1950
At the 4th annual Tony
Awards, *South Pacific*
receives eight, including
Best Musical of the Year
and a clean sweep of the
four acting categories —
a feat unparalleled in
Tony history.

10

11

1978
For three weeks during
the smash Broadway
revival of *The King and I*
the emphasis is taken off
the King and put back
on Anna when, at vacation
time, Angela Lansbury
steps in for Constance
Towers and Yul Brynner's
understudy, Michael
Kermoyan, takes over
for him.

Costume sketches by
Motley for South Pacific

12   13   14   15

1925
Rod Steiger is born in
Westhampton, New York.
Plays Jud Fry in the
movie version of
Oklahoma! (1955).

*Angela Lansbury in the
1978 Broadway revival of*
The King and I

16

17

18

1966
At the 38th annual
Academy Awards,
The Sound of Music
receives five Oscars,
including Best Picture
of the Year.

19

1945
Carousel opens at the
Majestic Theatre, New
York, where it runs for
890 performances.

Show poster for Carousel
(1945)

20   21   22   23

1953
The world premiere of
Me and Juliet is presented
at the Hanna Theatre,
Cleveland.

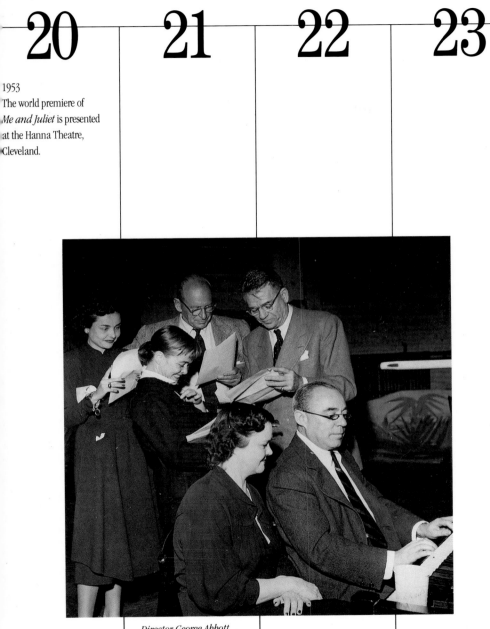

*Director George Abbott
(third from left),
Hammerstein and Rodgers
lead a rehearsal for* Me
and Juliet *(1953)*

24 25 26 27

1950
The national tour of
South Pacific opens at
the Hanna Theatre,
Cleveland, and tours for
five years, visiting 118
cities before closing at the
Chicago Opera House on
March 26, 1955.

1960
At the 14th annual Tony
Awards *The Sound of
Music* receives five, includ-
ing Best Actress (Mary
Martin) and, for the first
time in Tony history,
shares a tie for Best
Musical (with *Fiorello!*).

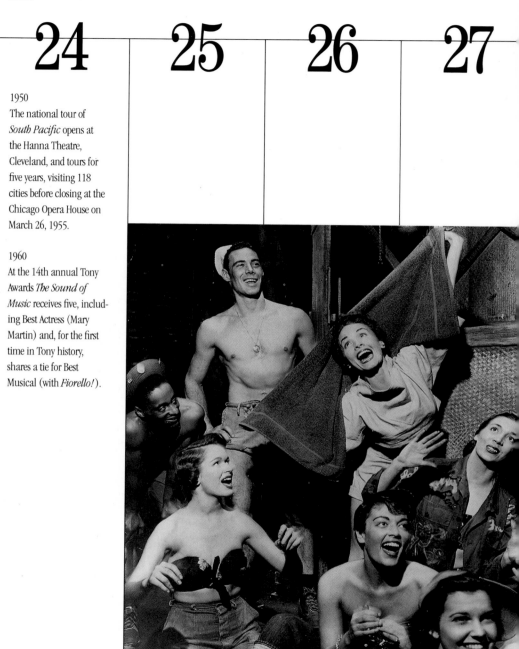

28

29

30

1919
Celeste Holm is born in
New York City. The original
Ado Annie in *Oklahoma!*,
she also stars in *The King
and I* on Broadway
(replacing Gertrude
Lawrence for two weeks
in 1952) and plays the
Fairy Godmother in
the 1965 television remake
of *Cinderella*.

1947
Oklahoma! opens at the
Theatre Royal, Drury Lane,
London, with Harold (later
Howard) Keel as Curly.

Celeste Holm in The King
and I *(1952)*

*Janet Blair with members
of the national touring
company of* South Pacific
(1950)

May

1

1950
South Pacific wins the
Pulitzer Prize for Drama.

1954
After ten-and-a-half years
on the road, the national
tour of *Oklahoma!* gives
its final performance
at the Shubert Theatre in
Philadelphia, thereby
bringing to a close the
longest Broadway road
tour in U.S. theatrical
history. In its decade-plus
run, the tour visits every
state in the union and
plays before a combined
audience of ten million.

2

1944
Oklahoma! is awarded
a special Pulitzer Prize
for Drama.

1977
Broadway's first revival of
The King and I, starring
Yul Brynner and Constance
Towers, opens at the Uris
Theatre, New York, and
runs for 695 performances.

3

4   5   6   7

1953
The Oklahoma State
Senate ratifies House
Bill #1094 declaring
"Oklahoma" to be "the
official song and anthem
of the state of Oklahoma."

Principals of Oklahoma!
*(1943): left to right, Lee
Dixon, Celeste Holm,
Alfred Drake, Joan Roberts
and Joseph Buloff
(kneeling)*

8 9 10 11

1960
The national tour of
Flower Drum Song begins
at the Riviera Theatre,
Detroit and plays in
twenty-two cities before
closing at the Hanna
Theatre, Cleveland,
on October 14, 1961.

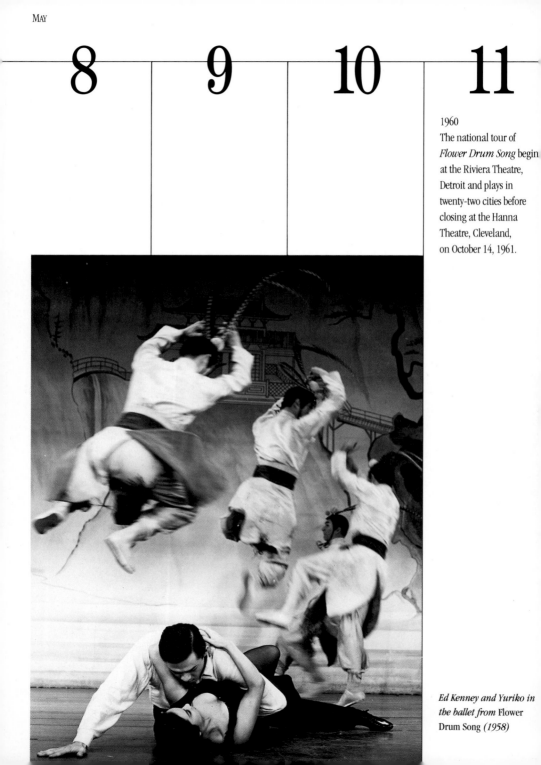

*Ed Kenney and Yuriko in
the ballet from* Flower
Drum Song *(1958)*

12

13

14

15

1955
Edward R. Murrow
interviews Oscar
Hammerstein II at his
townhouse in New York
City on "Person to Person,"
live on CBS-TV.

16 17 18 19

1946
Irving Berlin's musical
Annie Get Your Gun,
presented by Rodgers &
Hammerstein and starring
Ethel Merman, opens at
the Imperial Theatre,
New York, and runs for
1,147 performances.

1892
Ezio Pinza is born in
Rome, Italy. Creates the
role of Emile de Becque in
South Pacific (1949) and
receives the Tony Award
for his performance.

1961
The Sound of Music opens
at the Palace Theatre,
London.

*Mary Martin and Ezio
Pinza in* South Pacific
(1949)

20 21 22 23

Show poster for Me and Juliet *(1953)*

28

1953

Me and Juliet opens at
the Majestic Theatre,
New York, where it runs
for 358 performances.

29

1947

The national tour of
Carousel begins at the
Shubert Theatre in
Chicago and closes on
February 22, 1949, at the
Majestic Theatre, New York
(return engagement), after
an 88-week, 44-city tour.

1948

Oklahoma! closes on
Broadway after a
marathon five-year run of
2,212 performances.

30

31

1948

The Broadway company
of *Oklahoma!* opens at the
Boston Opera House at the
start of its year-long 67-city
national tour.

June

1

1951
After more than 900 performances, Mary Martin gives her final performance in *South Pacific* on Broadway.

2

1969
Ozzie and Harriet Nelson star in the stage premiere of Rodgers & Hammerstein's movie musical *State Fair*, at the St. Louis Municipal Opera.

3

4 5 6 7

1958
Ian Clayton and David
Atkinson head the cast of
Carousel, presented at the
American Theatre of
the U.S. Pavilion at the
Brussels World's Fair.

1950
Carousel opens at the
Theatre Royal, Drury
Lane, London, where it
runs for 566 performances.

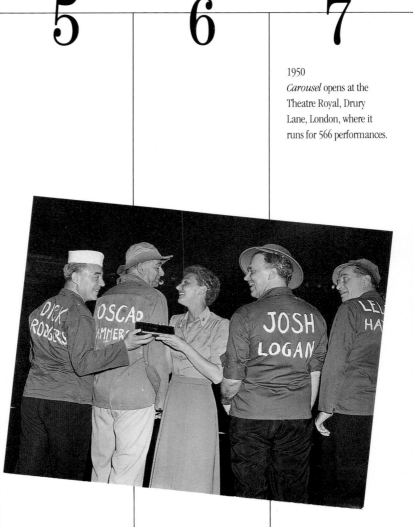

*Coproducers Rodgers,
Hammerstein, Joshua
Logan, and Leland
Hayward, with Mary
Martin after her final
Broadway performance in
South Pacific (1951)*

8 9 10 11

Sheet music cover for
Carousel *(1945)*

12

1979
Paul Brynner and Virginia
McKenna star in a revival
of *The King and I* at
London's Palladium
Theatre, running until
September 27, 1980.

13

14

15

1963
The Sound of Music closes
at the Mark Hellinger
Theatre, New York, after
1,443 performances.

*"June is Bustin' Out All
Over"* from the film
Carousel *(1956)*

16 17 18 19

1944
Williamson Music publishes "We're on Our Way," written by Rodgers & Hammerstein and dedicated to the U.S. Army Infantry.

20   21   22   23

1955
Oklahoma! is presented at
Théâtre des Champs
Elysées in Paris as part of
the American National
Theatre and Academy
"Salute to France" festival,
with a cast headed by Jack
Cassidy as Curly and
Shirley Jones as Laurey.

*Mary Martin with Dorothy
and Richard Rodgers at his
surprise birthday party,
June 25, 1950*

24   25   26   27

From left to right: Rita Moreno, Martin Benson, Deborah Kerr, and Yul Brynner, in the film The King and I *(1956)*

28

1902
Richard Charles Rodgers is born in New York City.

1956
Twentieth Century Fox releases the movie version of *The King and I*, starring Deborah Kerr, Yul Brynner, and Rita Moreno.

29

30

1985
At the Broadway Theatre, New York, Yul Brynner gives his 4,625th and final performance as the King in *The King and I*. At his curtain call Brynner is serenaded by the cast and audience with "Auld Lang Syne" and a letter is read from President Ronald Reagan. It is estimated that in 34 years of performing the King on the American stage, Brynner has been seen by three-and-a-half million people on Broadway and four-and-a-half million more on the road.

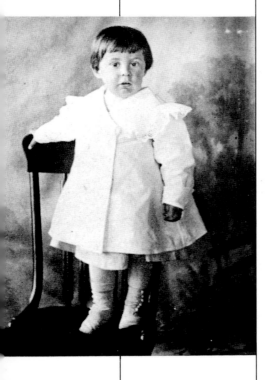

Richard Rodgers, age one

July

1

1946
Oklahoma! surpasses
Hellzapoppin's run of
1,404 performances to
become the longest
running show in Broadway
history, a record it holds
until *My Fair Lady*
surpasses it fifteen
years later.

2

3

1985
Variety reports that the
final week of Yul Brynner's
farewell engagement in
The King and I at the
Broadway Theatre, New
York, sets an all-time
Broadway box office
record of $605,546 —
the highest single-week
(eight-performance) tally
in Broadway history.

4

1898
Gertrude Lawrence is born in London. Creates the role of Anna in *The King and I* (1951), earning the Tony award for her performance.

5

1964
Director Robert Wise and his *Sound of Music* cast and crew wrap up eleven weeks of shooting on location in and around Salzburg, Austria.

6

7

Gertrude Lawrence prepares for a television appearance with Rodgers and Hammerstein (1951)

8

9

1955
Following its appearance
in Paris, the ANTA-spon-
sored tour of *Oklahoma!*
is presented at the Teatro
Quattro Fontanne in Rome,
followed by engagements
in Milan, Naples, and
Venice.

10

11

Julie Andrews and the children in the film The Sound of Music *(1965)*

Aunt Eller's farmhouse, on location for the film Oklahoma! *(1955)*

12

1895
Oscar Greeley Clendenning
Hammerstein (Oscar
Hammerstein II) is born
in New York City.

13

14

1954
Location shooting for
the movie version of
Oklahoma! begins in
Nogales, Arizona.

15

1922
Joan Roberts, the original
Laurey in *Oklahoma!*
(1943), is born in
New York City.

*Oscar Hammerstein II, age
twelve*

16

17

18

19

1955
St. Louis Municipal Opera
kicks off a six-week
"Rodgers & Hammerstein
Festival" featuring a
Rodgers & Hammerstein
symphony concert and
productions of *Carousel*,
Allegro, *The King and I*,
and *South Pacific*.

Oklahoma! *in Tel Aviv*
(1982)

20 21 22 23

1942
In the first public announcement of a Rodgers & Hammerstein musical, *The New York Times* reports: "The Theatre Guild announced yesterday that Richard Rodgers, Lorenz Hart and Oscar Hammerstein II will soon begin work on a musical version of Lynn Riggs' folk-play *Green Grow the Lilacs*."

Oklahoma! *in Oslo (1988)*

24 25 26 27

1976
A revival of *The King and I*
starring Yul Brynner opens
at the Starlight Theatre
in Indianapolis and closes
at the Westbury Music Fair
in New York on October 2,
1976. Its success leads to
a triumphant Broadway
revival the following
spring.

Sheet music cover (1953)

28 29 30 31

1953
MGM releases the movie
Main Street to Broadway,
featuring a host of
Broadway celebrities in
cameo appearances.
In one sequence,
Richard Rodgers, Oscar
Hammerstein II, Joshua
Logan, and Mary Martin
play themselves "in
rehearsal" for a new
musical, during which
Martin sings "There's
Music in You," written by
Rodgers & Hammerstein
especially for the film.

1944
Williamson Music
publishes "Dear Friend,"
a song by Rodgers &
Hammerstein. All
proceeds go to the 5th
War Loan Drive.

August

1   2   3

4 5 6 7

1948
The New York Philharmonic Symphony Orchestra presents its first "Rodgers & Hammerstein Night" at Lewisohn Stadium in New York. A crowd of 20,000 attends and the R & H concerts become annual season finales at the stadium for more than a decade, with Richard Rodgers serving frequently as guest conductor.

Gertrude Lawrence and Yul Brynner in The King and I *(1951)*

8

9

10

11

1955
The advance team from
Twentieth Century Fox
arrives in Boothbay Harbor,
Maine, to begin preproduc-
tion work on the movie
version of *Carousel*. It is
announced that Judy
Garland and Frank Sinatra
will star, but she drops out
prior to filming and he
less than two weeks into
the shoot. They are
replaced by Shirley Jones
and Gordon MacRae.

*Mitzi Gaynor (center) and
nurses on location for the
film* South Pacific *(1958)*

12

13

14

15

1957
Principal photography for
the movie of *South Pacific*
begins at Lihue on the
Hawaiian island of Kauai.

Oklahoma!'s Ado Annie
chooses this day for her
wedding. *"Will Parker:*
Why August fifteenth? *Ado:*
That was the first day I was
kissed. *Will:* Was it? I didn't
remember that. *Ado:* You
wasn't there."

16

17

18

1989
Rudolf Nureyev stars in
a six-month national
touring revival of *The King
and I,* beginning at the
Syracuse, New York,
Civic Center.

19

1980
Yul Brynner gives his
3,000th performance as
the King during a revival
of *The King and I* at the
Palladium Theatre,
London.

20

21

1955
Eddie Fisher, Shirley Jones, Ed Sullivan, Richard Rodgers, Oscar Hammerstein II and the governors of New York and Oklahoma lead an "Oklahoma Song-Fest" at the Central Park Mall in New York before a crowd of 15,000.

22

1917
Oscar Hammerstein II marries Myra Finn; they are divorced in 1929.

23

1960
Oscar Hammerstein II dies at his farm in Doylestown, Pennsylvania, at the age of 65.

1990
In celebration of *The Sound of Music*'s silver anniversary, Twentieth Century Fox hosts a gala screening/reunion for director Robert Wise, star Julie Andrews, and other members of the cast in Los Angeles; the movie is subsequently rereleased for a limited engagement in Los Angeles and New York.

A 1990 family reunion of the film The Sound of Music: *from left to right, Angela Cartwright, Charmian Carr, Kym Karath, Julie Andrews, director Robert Wise, Debbie Turner, Heather Menzies, and Duane Chase*

24

1945
The world premiere of
Rodgers & Hammerstein's
movie musical *State Fair*
is presented at the
Paramount Theatre,
Des Moines, Iowa.

25

26

1917
Jan Clayton, the original
Julie Jordan in *Carousel,*
is born in Alamogordo,
New Mexico.

27

*Jan Clayton and John Raitt
in* Carousel *(1945)*

28   29   30   31

1953
The national tour of
Oklahoma! begins a week
of performances at the New
York City Center, joining
*South Pacific, The King
and I,* and *Me and Juliet,*
already running on
Broadway, and prompting
New York City Mayor
Vincent R. Impelliteri
to proclaim "Rodgers &
Hammerstein Week."

Movie poster (1950)

September

1

1960

At the request of New York City Mayor Robert F. Wagner, the lights in the Broadway theatre district are temporarily blacked out at 9:00 P.M. in memory of Oscar Hammerstein II.

2

1967

Oklahoma! opens at the Takarazuka Theatre, Tokyo, with an all-female cast.

3

1947

The world premiere of *Allegro* is presented at the Shubert Theatre in New Haven.

John Battles (seated down stage) and John Conte (seated upstage), feature in Allegro *(1947)*

8   9   10   11

Yul Brynner in the film
The King and I *(1956)*

12

1951
The national tour of
Oklahoma! goes interna-
tional with a two-week
engagement at the Berlin
International Theatre
Festival's Titania Palast.

13

1983
Dorothy Rodgers and
Dorothy Hammerstein
host a party in Los Angeles
for Yul Brynner on the
occasion of his 4,000th
performance as the King
in *The King and I.*

14

15

16   17   18   19

1902
Agnes George de Mille is
born in New York City.
Choreographs *Oklahoma!*
(1943), *Carousel* (1945),
directs and choreographs
Allegro (1947), and choreographs the movie
version of *Oklahoma!*
(1955).

20

991
he movie of *The King
nd I* is shown outdoors
the Hollywood Bowl on
e world's largest movie
reen as part of American
nematheque's annual
"Movies at the Bowl"
ent. Mary Rodgers and
mes Hammerstein, a
ughter and son of the
uthors, introduce the film
a crowd of 18,000.

21

22

23

mes de Mille's dream
llet from* Oklahoma!
943)

24

25

26

27

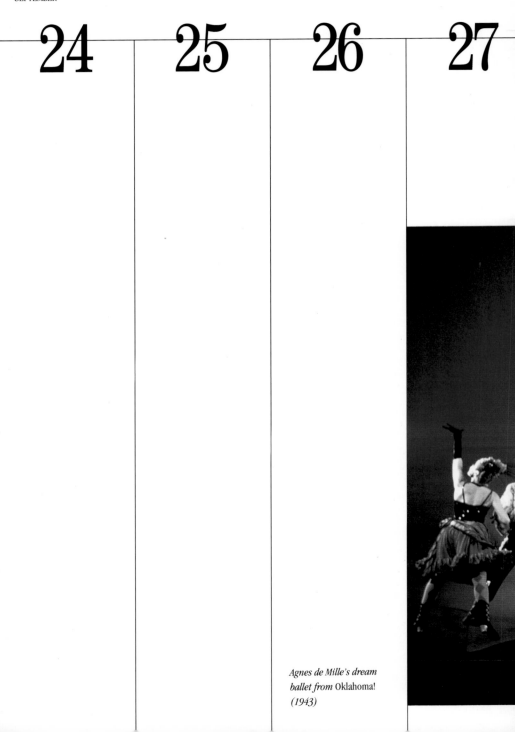

*Agnes de Mille's dream
ballet from* Oklahoma!
(1943)

28   29   30

October

1

1935
Julie Andrews is born
in Walton-on-Thames,
Surrey, England. Stars in
the television premiere of
Cinderella (1957), the
movie version of *The
Sound of Music* (1965),
and a studio recording of
The King and I (1992).

2

3

1959
The world premiere of
The Sound of Music is
presented at the Shubert
Theatre, New Haven.

*Julie Andrews in the
summer of 1964 on the
film set of* The Sound of
Music

4 5 6 7

1908
Joshua Logan is born
in Texarkana, Texas.
Coproduces, coauthors,
and directs *South Pacific*
(1949).

1914
Alfred Drake is born in New
York City. The original
Curly in *Oklahoma!,* he
turns down an offer to
create the role of the King
in *The King and I,* but for
three months in 1952 he
replaces Yul Brynner in
that part on Broadway.

*Joshua Logan, Rodgers,
and Hammerstein in
rehearsal for* South Pacific
(1949)

8

1897
Rouben Mamoulian is born in Tiflis, Georgia, Russia. Directs *Oklahoma!* (1943) and *Carousel* (1945).

1953
Valerie Hobson and Herbert Lom star in the London premiere of *The King and I,* which opens at the Theatre Royal, Drury Lane, and runs for 926 performances.

9

10

1947
Allegro opens at the Majestic Theatre, New York, where it runs for 315 performances.

11

1918
Jerome Robbins is born in New York City. Choreographs *The King and I* on stage (1951) and screen (1956).

1955
The movie version of *Oklahoma!* is released, presented by Rodgers & Hammerstein, directed by Fred Zinneman, and starring Gordon MacRae, Shirley Jones, Gloria Grahame, and Rod Steiger.

Alfred Drake and Joan Roberts in Oklahoma! *(1943)*

12   13   14   15

1943
The national tour of
Oklahoma! opens
at the Shubert Theatre,
New Haven.

1959
Oscar Hammerstein II
begins work on "Edelweiss,"
his 1,589th and last lyric,
written for *The Sound of
Music*. It is completed on
October 21 and goes into
the show during its pre-
Broadway tryout in Boston.

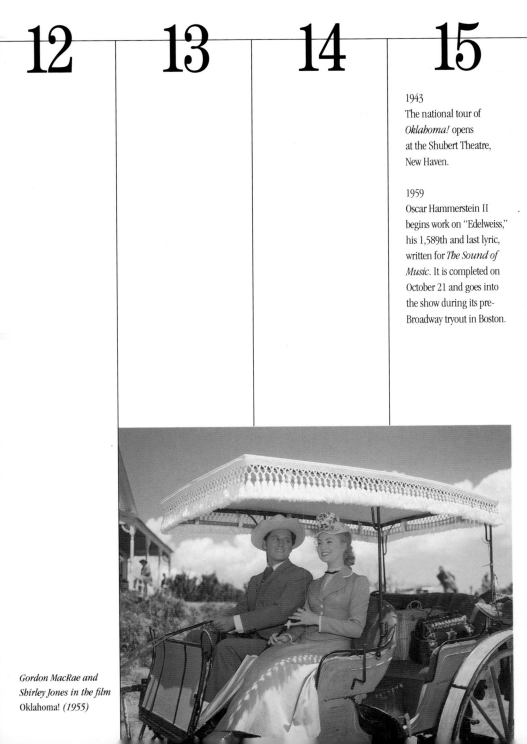

*Gordon MacRae and
Shirley Jones in the film*
Oklahoma! *(1955)*

16 17 18 19

1944
John van Druten's play
I Remember Mama,
presented by Rodgers &
Hammerstein, opens at
the Music Box Theatre,
New York, and runs for
714 performances.

1950
John Steinbeck's play
Burning Bright,
presented by Rodgers &
Hammerstein, opens at
the Broadhurst Theatre,
New York, and runs for
13 performances.

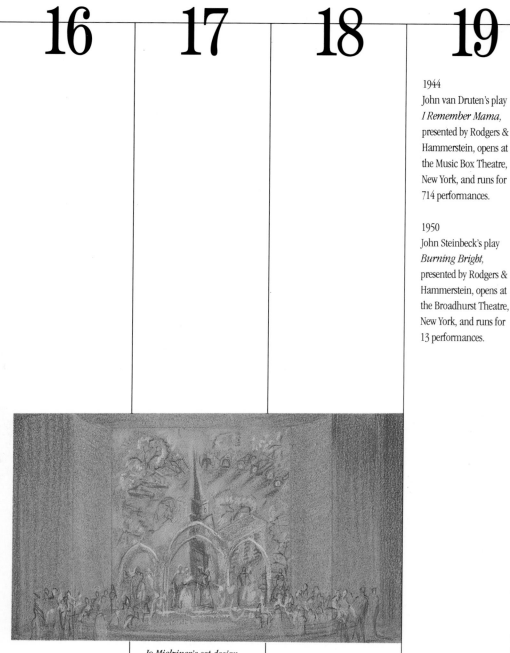

*Jo Mielziner's set design
for* Allegro *(1947)*

20

1947

Time magazine profiles Oscar Hammerstein II with a cover story entitled "The Careful Dreamer."

21

1950

Oklahoma! closes at the Theatre Royal, Drury Lane, London, after 1,548 performances, making it then the longest-running show in the 287-year history of the Drury Lane.

22

1955

The world premiere of *Pipe Dream* is presented at the Shubert Theatre, New Haven.

23

Helen Traubel, Judy Tyler, and William Johnson (trio, left of the telescope) head the cast of Pipe Dream *(1955)*

24

25

26

27

1958
The world premiere of
Flower Drum Song is
presented at the Shubert
Theatre, Boston.

28

29

30

31

1946
Anita Loos' comedy *Happy
Birthday,* presented by
Rodgers & Hammerstein
and starring Helen Hayes,
opens at the Broadhurst
Theatre, New York, and
runs for 564 performances.
In the play Helen Hayes
sings "I Haven't Got a
Worry in the World,"
written especially for her
by the producers.

*Rodgers and Hammerstein
in Boston, 1947*

November

1

1951
Mary Martin and Wilbur
Evans star in the London
premiere of *South Pacific*,
which opens at the Theatre
Royal, Drury Lane, and
plays for 802 performances.

2

3

4   **5**   **6**   **7**

1948
The national tour of
Allegro opens at the
Shubert Theatre, Phila-
delphia, at the start of a
31-week, 16-city tour.

1901
Juanita Hall is born in
Keyport, New Jersey.
Creates the roles of Bloody
Mary in *South Pacific*
(1949; Tony Award) and
Madam Liang in *Flower
Drum Song* (1958) and
re-creates both roles in the
movie versions (1958 and
1961, respectively).

1953
Edward R. Murrow inter-
views Richard and Dorothy
Rodgers live from their
Manhattan home on
"Person to Person,"
CBS-TV.

rance Nuyen, Juanita
all, and John Kerr in the
lm South Pacific *(1958)*

8   9   10   11

1961
Universal Pictures releases
the movie version of
Flower Drum Song,
produced by Ross Hunter
and starring Nancy Kwan,
Miyoshi Umeki, Jack Soo,
James Shigeta, and Juanita
Hall. Marilyn Horne dubs
the song "Love Look Away."

12   13   14   15

1954
At Carnegie Hall, New York,
Richard Rodgers leads the
New York Philharmonic
Symphony Orchestra in a
concert of his works.

*Mary Martin, seen from the
wings in* The Sound of
Music *(1959)*

*Miyoshi Umeki and James
Shigeta in the film* Flower
Drum Song *(1961)*

16   17   18   19

1907
Oklahoma becomes the
46th state in the union.

1959
The Sound of Music opens
at the Lunt-Fontanne
Theatre, New York.

*Mary Martin and children
in* The Sound of Music
(1959)

20 21 22 23

24 25 26 27

1946
The first performance of
Oklahoma! in the state of
Oklahoma is presented at
the Municipal Auditorium
in Oklahoma City. Gover-
nor Robert S. Kerr presides
over several days of state-
wide celebrations, joined
by Rodgers, Hammerstein,
their wives, and members of
the musical's creative team.
Rodgers & Hammerstein
are made honorary
members of the Kiowa
Indian tribe.

28   29   30

1955
Pipe Dream opens
at the Shubert Theatre,
New York, and runs for
246 performances.

1965
The Rodgers &
Hammerstein Archives
of Recorded Sound
open to the public at the
Performing Arts Research
Center of the New York
Public Library. Featured in
this general collection are
approximately 500,000
recordings from the late
19th century to the present.

Show poster (1955)

December

1

1913
Mary Martin is born in Weatherford, Texas. Creates the roles of Nellie Forbush in *South Pacific* and Maria von Trapp in *The Sound of Music,* winning a Tony Award for each.

1958
Flower Drum Song opens at the St. James Theatre, New York, and runs for 600 performances.

2

1943
Decca releases the original cast album of *Oklahoma!,* the first comprehensive original Broadway cast album.

1947
Oklahoma! gives its 2,000th performance on Broadway. Composer Richard Rodgers is on hand to conduct the second act.

3

Miyoshi Umeki in Flower Drum Song *(1958)*

4 5 6 7

1909
The world premiere of Ferenc Molnar's play *Liliom* is presented at the Vigszínház Theatre, Budapest. It is produced in New York several times with several different translations (one allegedly written by Lorenz Hart) before Rodgers & Hammerstein adapt the Benjamin Glazer text as their basis for *Carousel*.

Rodgers conducts the 2,000th performance of Oklahoma! *on Broadway (1947)*

8 9 10 11

12

13

14

15

1979
With Governor George
Nigh of Oklahoma
among the dignitaries
in attendance, a revival
of *Oklahoma!* directed
by Hammerstein's son,
William, opens at
Broadway's Palace
Theatre. Preceded by
a six-month tour, it
plays on Broadway for
293 performances before
going out on another
national tour.

Oklahoma! *in its 1979*
Broadway revival

16 17 18 19

1958
The stage premiere of
Rodgers & Hammerstein's
television musical
Cinderella is presented
by Harold Fielding at
London's Coliseum in
the style of a traditional
English pantomime with
Tommy Steele as the star.

*Gordon MacRae and
Shirley Jones in the film*
Carousel *(1956)*

20 21 22 23

1950
The national tour of *Oklahoma!,* in its seventh year, opens in Cheyenne, Wyoming — thereby achieving the feat of having performed in every state in the union.

Betta St. John and William Tabbert in South Pacific *(1949)*

24   25   26   27

THE EDITORS OF LIFE PRESENT
THE FIRST PUBLICATION ANYWHERE OF A NEW SONG:

Happy Christmas,
Little Friend

WORDS BY
Oscar
Hammerstein, 2nd

MUSIC BY
Richard
Rodgers

Roger Duvoisin

From Life *magazine (1952)*

28

29

1952

Life magazine publishes Rodgers & Hammerstein's only Christmas song, "Happy Christmas Little Friend," commissioned by the magazine as a gift for its readers. In 1953 it is designated the official Christmas Seal sale song.

30

1979

Richard Rodgers dies at his home in New York City at the age of 77.

31

1979

CBS presents a special tribute to Richard Rodgers on the night following his death. Commentator Charles Kuralt eulogizes, "He was a composer for the 1920s and then, it turned out, he was a composer for the thirties, the forties, the fifties and the sixties too, and on the last night of the seventies we say goodbye to him. Not to his music — that will go on and on and on in our theatres and in our heads."

Photograph Credits

Special thanks to Philip Pocock who photographed original photographs and artwork.

The Billy Rose Theatre Collection, New York Public Library for the Performing Arts, Astor, Lenox and Tilden Foundations: page 2, April 24–28 (Alfredo Valente), May 4–7 (Vandamm), May 24–27, Sept. 16–19 (Vandamm), Nov. 19–23;

The Bob Golby Collection, Theatre Arts Collection, Harry Ransom Humanities Research Center, The University of Texas at Austin: April 4–7;

CBS: Feb. 20–23, July 4–7;

Courtesy of The Rodgers and Hammerstein Organization: pages 4–11, Jan. 12–15, Feb. 1–3, Feb. 11–15, Feb. 16–19, Feb. 20–23, Feb. 28–29, March 4–7, March 11–15, March 24–27, April 8–11, April 20–23, April 28–30, May 20–23, June 4–7, June 8–30, July 11, July 12–15, July 16–23, Aug. 11–15, Aug. 28–31, Sept. 8, Oct. 12, Oct. 16–19, Oct. 20–23, Oct. 24–27, Nov. 12–15, Nov. 24, Nov. 28–30, Dec. 4–7, Dec. 24–27;

© Eileen Darby: 16–19, Aug. 24–27, Sept. 4–7;

Franks Driggs Collection: July 24–27;

Drawing by Roger Duvoisin: Dec. 24–27;

Toni Frissell, Theatre Collection Museum of the City of New York: Jan. 8–11, Jan. 28–31;

Lester Glassner Collection/Neal Peters: Jan. 20–23;

© Henry Grossman: Jan. 1–4;

Peter Howard: Nov. 8–9;

The Kobal Collection: March 12, Oct. 12;

Gjon Mili, LIFE MAGAZINE © Time Warner Inc.: Sept. 27–30;

Photograph © Alan Berliner, Courtesy of The Rodgers and Hammerstein Organization: Aug. 16–19;

Photograph by Friedman-Abeles, Courtesy of The Rodgers and Hammerstein Organization: May 8–11, Dec. 1–3;

© Martha Swope: March 11–15, Dec. 8–11;

Theatre Collection Museum of the City of New York: April 16–19, Aug. 1–3 (Vandamm), Oct. 4–7.

Film Copyrights

Front Cover: *The King and I*, © 1956 Argyle Enterprises and Twentieth Century Fox Film Corporation. All Rights Reserved.

Back Cover: *The Sound of Music*, © 1965 Argyle Enterprises and Twentieth Century Fox Film Corporation. All Rights Reserved.

Pages 4–5: *State Fair*, © 1945 Argyle Enterprises and Twentieth Century Fox Film Corporation. All Rights Reserved.

Feb. 4–7: *The Sound of Music*, © 1965 Argyle Enterprises and Twentieth Century Fox Film Corporation. All Rights Reserved. *State Fair*, © 1962 Argyle Enterprises and Twentieth Century Fox Film Corporation. All Rights Reserved.

Feb. 12–15: *Carousel*, © 1956 Argyle Enterprises and Twentieth Century Fox Film Corporation. All Rights Reserved.

Feb. 16–19: *Carousel*, © 1956 Argyle Enterprises and Twentieth Century Fox Film Corporation. All Rights Reserved.

March 4–7: *The Sound of Music*, © 1965 Argyle Enterprises an Twentieth Century Fox Film Corporation. All Rights Reserved.

June 24–27: *The King and I*, © 1956 Argyle Enterprises and Twentieth Century Fox Film Corporation. All Rights Reserved.

July 11: *The Sound of Music*, © 1965 Argyle Enterprises and Twentieth Century Fox Film Corporation. All Rights Reserved.

July 12: *Oklahoma!*, Courtesy of The Rodgers and Hammerstein Organization.

Aug. 11–15: *South Pacific*, Courtesy of The Rodgers and Hammerstein Organization.

Aug. 28–31: *State Fair*, © 1945 Argyle Enterprises and Twentieth Century Fox Film Corporation. All Rights Reserved.

Sept. 8–11: *The King and I*, © 1956 Argyle Enterprises and Twentieth Century Fox Film Corporation. All Rights Reserved.

Oct. 1–3: *The Sound of Music*, © 1965 Argyle Enterprises an Twentieth Century Fox Film Corporation. All Rights Reserved.

Oct. 12–15: *Oklahoma!* Courtesy of The Rodgers and Hammerstein Organization.

Nov. 1–3: *South Pacific*, Courtesy of The Rodgers and Hammerstein Organization.

Nov. 8–11: *Flower Drum Song*, 1961, Copyright © by Universal Pictures, a Division of Universal City Studios, Inc. Courtesy of MCA Publishing Rights, a Division of MCA Inc.

Dec. 16–19: *Carousel*, © 1956 Argyle Enterprises and Twentieth Century Fox Film Corporation. All Rights Reserved.

Principal Sources

The Rodgers & Hammerstein Fact Book; © 1955 by Richard Rodgers and Oscar Hammerstein II; edited and revised by Stanley Green © 1980; Hal Leonard Publishing.

The Rodgers & Hammerstein Fact Book revised; © 1980 by The Lynn Farnol Group; edited by Stanley Green.

The Richard Rodgers Fact Book; © 1965, 1968 by The Lynn Farnol Group, Inc.

Getting to Know Him, The Biography of Oscar Hammerstein II © 1977 by Hugh Fordin; Random House, New York.

The Sound of Their Music; © 1978 by Frederick Nolan; J.M. Dent & Sons, Ltd., London.

Who's Who in the Theatre, Sixteenth Edition; © 1977 by Ian Herbert; Pitman Publishing Ltd., London.

Musical Stages, An Autobiography; © 1975 by Richard Rodgers; Random House, New York.

The Tony Award Book; © 1987 by Lee Alan Morrow; Abbeville Press, New York.

Fifty Golden Years of Oscar, The Official History of the Academy of Motion Picture Arts & Sciences; © 1979 by Robert Osborne; Ese California, La Habra, CA.

Who's Who in Show Business, Revised Edition; © 1985 Mike Kaplan, ed.; Garland Publishing, Inc; New York and London.